The Edge Of The Light

(Small Book)

Peter Blueberry

Thank you for the small things

that go un-noticed,

Olivia, Blake, Calvin, Dane, and Rose.

The Edge Of The Light *(Small book)*

© 2019 Peter Blueberry – Shadow version

www.peterblueberry.com

Library of Congress Control Number: 2017951579

Table of Contents

Shopping For An Ooblick

I smell Cherry Pie?

Shopping for an Ooblick
Is really quite a feat.
He'll insist on sitting . . .
. . . in the basket,
And sticking out his feet.

Chocolate milk and gingerbread,
Cereal, syrup, and gum,
Doughnuts and pretzels,
We've only just begun.

On and on we go
Until our basket is piled high.
Until nothings left in the store
Except one lonely . . .
. . . cherry pie.

Then the Ooblick says,. . .
. . ."Don't worry,"
He says it loud and clear,
"Don't bother putting it. . .
. . .in a bag.
I'll just eat it all. . .
. . .right here."

Do you see what I see?

The Corn Field

There's a giant corn field
Out behind my house.
And I think it's where monsters grow.
I swear I saw a 2 ton mouse.

Now, I know there are other things out there
That I'm sure I think I've seen.
But if I've been looking at them,
Have they been looking at me?

5

It wasn't me this time.

Don't Look In The Box

Don't look in that box over there.
Don't you dare lift that lid.
There are three boys who didn't listen.
There are three boys who wished they did.

There is something in there
That will turn you into goo,
And if you lift the lid too high,
It will put its spell on you.

So, if you don't want to live
In that realm of in-between,
Keep your wits about you.
Tonight is Halloween.

Yucky

I see something yucky,
Something gooey on the floor.
It's dripping from my bathroom cabinet,
From the bottom of the drawer.
I don't want it on my clothes,
Or to drip onto my skin.
No telling what it is,
Or even where it's been.
I'll just open up the cabinet,
And take a look within.
Why, it's just my toothpaste.
I forgot to put the **cap on again.**

Now, what was I looking for?

Sea Creatures

If you go to the beach,
And are careful to look,
You'll find sea creatures hiding
In crannies and nooks.

They live in the sand,
And between the rocks.
Or inside a seashell.
Hey! Be careful where you walk.

This is their home,
This beach by the sea.
They don't mind if you look at them,
But, please **let them be.**

The Caterpillar

I'm looking at a caterpillar
  Outside my window pane,
    Crawling on a tree branch,
    Getting pelted by the rain.

    It doesn't seem to matter,
    It just keeps on inching along,
  But I sit here and wonder,
 "What keeps it **hanging on?**"

I'm going to be an astronaut!

Rocket Anny

She came in riding her skateboard,
Red hair flying behind her head.
All the girls were playing dress-up.
Anny wanted to climb instead.

They all thought Anny was strange
When she turned upside-down,
And did 6 one hand cart wheels,
And twirled 12 times around and around.

She swung out on a tree limb,
As high up as she pleased,
And started talking to the girls below,
While hanging by her knees.

"I'm going to be an Astronaut,"
Anny told them with a yawn,
"I'm going into space.
I'm going to the Moon and beyond."

The girls stopped what they were doing,
And gazed amazingly at Anny instead.
Then Anny shot off riding her skateboard,
Red hair flying behind her head.

And don't you know to think,
Anny's skateboard was pink.

"Um, does anybody have a toothpick?"

No Team

Barely the alligator
Didn't have much of a team.
There was no one on his side.
Not a team mate could be seen.

The other side had 12 players
Who were ready to play ball.
Barely said, "I guess I don't have a team,
Because I **ate them all."**

Molly Mack

My name is Molly Mack.
My favorite color is black,
And I love to play soccer at night.

But I didn't see
The ball coming at me.
Isn't my **black eye a beautiful sight?**

Molly Mac never ducks!

The Edge Of The Light

There are such things out there
That go lurking around.
Just when it gets dark.
They don't make a sound.

If they are really out there,
They don't stay for long.
You think that you...
...can see them.
But when you look there...
...they are gone.

These creatures live...
...in the shadows,
Just out of sight.
These creatures live
In Edge of the Light.

Privacy

It's nice of you
To want to play,
And stay with me
Throughout the day.

Show me your frog
A little bit later,
Your marble collection,
And stuffed alligator.

But for now,
As you can see,
I'm going to the…
…bathroom.
Please! Give me some…
… privacy.

Text me - Dude!

I take it back! I take it back!

Don't Ask

Dinosaurs are enormous,
Ungainly and clumsy.
They have really big feet.
They're awkward and...
...bumbly.

They'll sit and play...
...checkers
All day long.
Yahtzee, Old Maid,
And sometime Mahjong.

As long as they're ...
... sitting,
Dinosaurs are O.K.
But when they get up
They can ruin your day.

So, be very careful,
And don't take ...
... a chance,
And never, never, ...
... never,
Ask a dinosaur ...
... **to dance.**

19

That's cloud #3,000,000,000,000 and 3!

The Sky Scraper

I'm a Sky Scraper,
And I clean the skies,
Scrubbing the clouds
As they float by.

I take pride in my work,
And I'm good at what I do.
I've been cleaning clouds
Since 19-0-2.

But it's getting much harder
To clean off the gunk,
Because people keep making
Mountains of junk.

They make an abundance
Of doohickeys today,
They use them once,
Then throw them away.

Now, all of this mess
Will get into the air,
Just think of the sky,
And please say you care.

So, send me some help.
I'm falling behind,
And please use your doohickeys
More than one time.

Billy Grant

Billy Grant walked with a slant.
  His shoes were worn out on one side.
    One arm hung short and the other one long,
      And Billy couldn't walk up straight if he tried.

          He was looking for some place
            Where his slant would be at home.
              He was tired of being different,
                And he was tired of being alone.

                    So Billy walked and walked...
                      ...and walked,
                        And then he . . .
                          . . . walked some more.
                            His feet were . . .
                              . . . getting tired,
                                And on one side . . .
                                  . . . they were getting sore.

Then Billy found a village
In a valley on its side,
And everybody in there
Had their shoes worn out...
... on one side.

All the people of the village said,
"Billy, we like your slant,
Because walking up straight here
Is something that we can't."

"So, why don't you come and make
This valley your new home?"
Then Billy said, "Yes. I think I will."
Now Billy wasn't **alone.**

Hey! Is that a town on its side?

What Will I Become

If I didn't want to be myself,
What other would I be?
If I could change what I was,
What would people see?

> I could become a magnificent bird,
> And fly up high and free.
> Or, I could become a dashing pirate,
> And sail the seven seas.

Or, I could become something truly scary,
Or something really weird.
Or, I could become a cunning old wizard
With a 12 foot long white beard.

> But, if I had to give up my birthdays,
> And I couldn't have any more friends,
> And if I wouldn't get any more...
> ...Christmas presents,
> And my fun would have to end,

Would I give all this up to change,
And become something else?
Maybe it's better to stay what I am,
And just become myself.

This sword really fits me.

That's far enough! I've already enough problems without you sliming around!

The Closet

There's something in my closet.
I know I saw something move.
I think it dripped onto the floor,
And oozed into a groove.
It could slide under the door,
And slip over to my bed.
It could slime up my arm,
And try to eat my head.
So, just in case there's something in there,
I'll just creep over and close the door,
And try not to make a sound
As I nail it to the floor.

O.K. Who put this wall right here?

Awkward Ed

Awkward Ed
Bumped his head
Into the kitchen door.
A bump showed up
The size of a nut.
"This has happened to me before."
He turned around,
While sporting a frown,
And said, "This is not fair at all."
"I'd better be alert,
Or I might get hurt."
Then Ed walked straight **into the wall.**

I need to skip this!

Skipping

My name is Peg Slip,
And I love to skip.
I skip at least 50 . . .
. . . times a day.

I skip to school.
I'm a skipping fool,
"I'm skipping, please . . .
. . . clear the way."

Now, when Peg skips by
People say, "Oh my.
Move over. Let Peg . . .
. . . skip on through."

"She's such a cheerful child.
Just watch her a while,
And you'll want to start...
...skipping too."

Then it happened one day,
I heard Miss Dora Smith say,
"I haven't seen much of...
...Skipping Peg."

But you'll see her again.
Do you want to know when?
As soon as she gets . . .
. . . the cast off her leg.

Excuse me!
My allergies are sure acting up.

My Pet Dragon

I have a pet dragon.
His name is Agamemnon,
And he breathes fire,
When he turns his heat on.

He's 4 inches tall,
And I keep him in my underwear drawer.
But, that's O.K.,
Because I don't have . . .
. . . **underwear anymore.**

Fairies

Fairies ride
  On dragonflies.
    I saw one once
      From the corner of my eye.

        But they're hard to see,
          And you have to be quick.
            They're almost invisible,
            They're fast and they're swift.

          Their hair, it sparkles,
          Their wings are fair,
        And a trail of Fairy Dust
      They leave in the air.

But they're not to be followed,
  And they're not to be found.
    Just be happy
      That they're still around.

        And whenever you see
          A dragonfly,
            Just know that a fairy
            Is somewhere close by.

Justine! Hurry!
There's a meeting
in the Fairy's
Meadow today,
And I can't
be late <u>again</u>!

QUESTIONS

4. SHOPPING FOR AN OOBLICK
   A. Where are the Ooblick's feet? *Sticking out of the shopping basket*
   B. What does he do with all the food? *Eat it all right there*
5. THE CORN FIELD
   A. What did the boy think he saw? *A two ton mouse*
6. DON'T LOOK IN THE BOX
   A. What happened to the three boys? *They were turned into goo*
   B. What is tonight? *Halloween*
7. YUCKY
   A. Where is the goo dripping from? *The bottom of the drawer*
   B. What did he leave the cap off of? *The toothpaste*
8. SEA CREATURES
   A. Where do sea creatures hide? *In crannies and nooks*
10. THE CATERPILLAR
    A. What is the caterpillar crawling on? *A tree branch*
    B. What does the person wonder? *What keeps it hanging on*
12. ROCKET ANNY
    A. What is Anny riding? *A skateboard*
    B. Where is Anny going? *To the Moon and beyond*
    C. What color is Anny's skateboard? *Pink*
14. NO TEAM
    A. Where is Barely's team? *In his stomach*
15. MOLLY MACK
    A. What is Molly's favorite sport? *Soccer*
16. THE EDGE OF THE LIGHT
    A. How many monsters? *6*
18. PRIVACY
    A. What is the boy doing? *Going to the bathroom*
19. DON'T ASK
    A. Don't ask a dinosaur to what? *To dance*

20. THE SKYSCRAPER
    A. What does he do? *Scrubs the clouds as they float by*
    B. What does he want us to do with our doohickeys? *Use them more than one time*
    C. He's been cleaning clouds since when? *1902*
22. BILLY GRANT
    A. Where were Billy's shoes worn out? *On one side*
    B. Where was the town he found? *In a valley on its side*
24. WHAT WILL I BECOME
    A. He could become a dashing what? *Pirate*
    B. What didn't he want to give up? *Birthdays*
26. THE CLOSET
    A. Where did the thing ooze into? *A groove*
    B. What might it do if it slimed up his arm? *Eat his head*
27. AWKWARD ED
    A. What did Ed walk straight into? *The wall*
28. SKIPPING
    A. What is the girl's name? *Peg Slip*
    B. What happened to her leg? *She broke it*
29. MY PET DRAGON
    A. How tall is the dragon? *4 inches*
    B. Where does he keep his pet dragon? *In his underwear drawer*
    C. What happened to all the underwear? *They burned up*
30. FAIRIES
    A. What do Fairies ride on? *Dragonflies*
    B. What do fairies leave in the air? *A trail of fairy dust*
    C. What do you know if you see a dragonfly? *That a Fairy is somewhere close by*

www.ingramcontent.com/pod-product-compliance
Lightning Source LLC
Chambersburg PA
CBHW060554030426
42337CB00019B/3545